One De

MW00399301

Healthy Self-Esteem
To Go!!

One Deluxe Order Of

Healthy Self-Esteem
To Go!!

An easy to follow recipe for
positive self-esteem.

• • • • • • •

Six simple ingredients that will
provide you and your children
with a lifetime supply of
healthy self-esteem!

Billie Bacon

One Deluxe Order Of Healthy Self-Esteem To Go!!

An easy to follow recipe for positive self-esteem.

Six simple ingredients that will provide you and your children with a lifetime supply of healthy self-esteem!

by Billie Bacon, M.Ed.

Printed in the United States of America

Cover design and text layout by
Ad Graphics, Tulsa, OK

ISBN: 0-9672971-0-9

Dedication

• • • • • • • • • • •

To my husband, Jerry
For his love, encouragement and confidence.

To my children, Chris and Craig
For their love and friendship, and for teaching me so much.

To my mother and in memory of my dear father
For their nuturing love and support.

Acknowledgments

• • • • • • • • • • • •

So many people have been instrumental in bringing this book to press. I am indebted to my two wonderful children and to the many precious children and caring teachers who have crossed my path over the years. The beautiful lessons I have learned through their hearts and words made this book possible.

My husband, Jerry, gave me the confidence to forge ahead with this project. His support, encouragement, creativity and positive attitude turned obstacles into opportunities!

My sincere thanks to Zig Ziglar for lending his expert advice, editing skills and kind words to this effort. Thanks also to Angela Williams for her contributions in the editing department.

Finally, I thank Jim and Barbara Weems at Ad Graphics for putting the final product together for me. They skillfully combine expertise with unlimited patience, kindness and enthusiasm. What a joy it was to work with them!

Table Of Contents

• • • • • • • • • • • •

Introduction
• • • • • • • • • • •

Before my husband and I were married, we dated long distance for a slow-moving two years. He was in Charleston, S. C. , 1200 miles away from my cozy little duplex in Edmond, Oklahoma.

During those exciting but lonely times, we engaged in nightly telephone "visits" that often lingered into the early morning hours. Our costly little chats frequently touched on deep, mind-boggling topics and, occasionally, even waxed philosophical!

One such evening, Jerry posed a question to me. "What do you think," he asked, "is the most prevalent problem or weakness common to all people?" Without hesitation, I replied, "poor self-esteem."

It has been said that self-esteem or self-worth is the mainspring which marks all of us; adults, children, males and females alike for lives of success or failure. That is a powerful declaration to make about any one quality! Experts agree, however, that the key ingredient for feeling self-confident, capable, responsible and happy ourselves and for rearing children who possess these attributes is high, positive self-esteem.

In the following chapters, I will share with you my simple, easy-to-follow, homespun recipe for a more positive self-worth. It has merely six ingredients. They have been compiled from many years of experience, observation and information-gathering as a parent and counselor.

So, prepare to embark on an entertaining journey of growth and self-enhancement!

"Self-esteem is the single greatest need facing the human race today."

– Robert H. Schuller

"For at the deepest level, all social, political, economic, religious, and even scientific problems relate to the private and collective need for positive pride, or healthy self-esteem."

– Robert H. Schuller

Chapter 1
• • • • • • • • • • • •

What Is
Self-Esteem?

What Is Self-Esteem?

• • • • • • • • • • •

W hat is this concept that has been credited with determining our success or failure in life? How do we define this quality that appears to wield so much power over our lives?

It is easily defined. Our self-esteem denotes how we feel about ourselves—how we feel about who we are, what we are doing in life right now and where we are headed.

Positive self-esteem is twofold. It is internal. I believe that I am capable and lovable simply because I exist. I am okay just because I am "me." But, how I feel about myself is also tied to an external component. I must also feel that I am worthwhile and of value because I have some control over the outside world. I have some power over those external circumstances that affect my life. I must also believe that I am capable of making a contribution to society. Our self-esteem is directly influenced from within ourselves, but it is also affected by how we think the world views us and by how we interact with others.

Unfortunately, a definition is the simplest flavoring in this mixture. The difficult task lies in learning how to actually grab hold of this elusive, "thing" called self-esteem and absorb it into our very being. Of course, an even more challenging feat is gifting our children with this strength.

What are the factors that determine the image we have of ourselves? As I stated in the introduction, I believe there are six significant ingredients that influence how we rate our worth.

As you blend each of these nutrients into your daily life, you will begin to enjoy the sweet taste of self-confidence, true happiness, greater productivity and, most importantly, you will really love who you have become. Please feel free to apply the steps toward a higher self-esteem to yourself, your children, your spouse, your company or even the community in which you live. For whether we are five or fifty-five years of age, one individual or a corporation, our needs, worries, fears and desires are much the same.

"True self-esteem is the result of a developmental process that begins with liking oneself, and ends with a sense of competence and ability."

– Ava L. Siegler

"There is no value-judgment more important to man – no factor more decisive in his psychological development and motivation – than the estimate he passes on himself."

– Nathaniel Branden

Chapter 2

Step 1:
Create And
Maintain
A Balance

Step 1:
Create And Maintain
A Balance
• • • • • • • • • • •

The first ingredient in this fail-proof recipe for a more positive self-esteem calls for creating and maintaining a balance in our lives. All of us, young and old, need a comfortable balance among the physical, emotional, social, spiritual and intellectual aspects of our daily lives. We should try to devote some portion of time each day to work, play, quiet, private time and to social activities. It is impossible, of course, to spend the same amount of time in hours or minutes on each area every day. For most of us, the work segment consumes at least eight hours of the day. This fact alone makes it even more crucial to carve out a portion of time each day for playing, socializing and being quiet.

I sometimes think we humans are a lot like washing machines. When a washing machine is off balance, it bangs, jumps around and bungles the job. The clothes are not washed, rinsed or wrung properly. Don't we react in the same way? We begin making mistakes more frequently; nothing seems to go right. We may notice that we are more clumsy and find ourselves failing at small, routine tasks. The more we fail, the more frustrated we become, and our self-esteem rapidly diminishes.

Some obvious behavior changes accompany this out-of-balance state. Crankiness, aggression, withdrawal or irritability might appear unannounced! We often experience fatigue, headaches, stomachaches, and a rise in blood pressure. Our eating and sleep patterns may change.

We might feel depressed, helpless, hopeless and dissatisfied. Adults usually begin to have problems at work, completing tasks and interacting with fellow workers.

Children often have similar difficulties at school and at home. Their grades suffer as do their personal relationships. We may see more temper tantrums, and nightmares may become more frequent.

When that washing machine is off balance and making those intolerable noises, we don't ignore it, do we? No, we lift the lid, rearrange the clothes and re-create its balance. This enables it to run smoothly once more. That strategy is the same one we should apply to ourselves and to our children.

Slow down, take a health break. Restructure your time and schedule to regain a balance among the many roles you play. Help your child get back on an even keel by listening to what he is saying and to his behavior. Then gently guide him in making changes.

Even very young children can be victims of this "lopsided" feeling. Barbara, a fellow counselor in Oklahoma, related an incident with her four year old daughter, Laura. She had picked Laura up from daycare and was looking forward to the exciting evening she had planned for the two of them! They were going to enjoy dinner at McDonald's and then take in story-time at the library. Much to mommy's disappointment, Laura's mood did not match hers. Laura was cranky and irritable. You know those times when nothing seems to please your child. The mere mention of story-time sent Laura into a frenzy! Barbara said that she could sense that Laura had had enough social interaction for the day and was craving some quiet, peaceful time. So, they went home, put on their pajamas, curled up and watched her favorite Disney video together in silence.

In my position as a school counselor, I often encountered children who were overly regimented and scheduled in structured activities. They arose each morning early, quickly ate a bowl of cereal and went to school for six or seven very controlled hours. Following school, they began their extracurricular events. A typical week might consist of soccer on Monday, karate on Tuesday, scouts on Wednesday and piano on Thursday. Then throw in an hour of homework each evening, and we have created an extremely unbalanced existence for our child. He has had no quiet time, no alone time, no periods for undirected, free play.

A 1997 study at the University of Michigan's Institute for Social Research found that our youngsters' free time was steadily decreasing. They found that children were spending more time doing homework and chores, running errands with their parents and participating in organized activities and less time in creative, unregulated play.

Everyone needs downtime to unwind and just "be" for awhile.

Quite often, as parents and teachers, we try to be everything to everybody. Guess who gets lost in the shuffle? We forget ourselves. Always remember to pencil in some time each day for that bubble bath or a walk on the beach. We need to nurture our whole person, not just the physical or just the emotional.

Here is a little exercise to check your balance. On a sheet of paper, write down every single activity in which you have participated in the last three days. Include eating, exercise, reading, work, etc. Then label each of these experiences as physical, emotional, social, spiritual or intellectual. How equally did you devote time to each area? If you have a much greater number of activities in one area than in another, it might be a warning signal that you need to do some readjusting of priorities.

* * *

Strive to achieve more of a balance one day at a time, and feelings of self-worth and contentment will begin to soothe that bruised and tattered self-image.

"Physical, Mental and Spiritual Health are all closely interwoven."

– Zig Ziglar

"The key to inner peace and happy living is high self-esteem, for it lies behind successful involvement with others."

– Dorothy Corkille Briggs

"Oft-times nothing profits more than self-esteem, grounded on just and right well managed."

– John Milton

"Kids need it (unstructured time) to recuperate from the more structured part of their day and to just veg out."

– Peter Sheras, Ph.D.

Chapter 3

• • • • • • • • • • • •

Step 2:
Lighten-up

Step 2:
Lighten-up
•••••••••••

The second step on this menu of positive feelings is to learn to lighten-up!

Most of us tend to be so hard on ourselves. We impose unrealistic performance goals, stringent guidelines and very strict rules for our lives. Then, what happens when we do not reach our goals, or we stray outside of our rigid boundaries? We feel like failures and engage in some "self-battering" and, of course, guilt. Each time this familiar scenario occurs, our self-worth plummets.

By the time Saturday rolled around, my "to-do" list used to number in the double digits. I do not remember ever being able to check off all of the items on that list. So, at least half of the errands and chores would be bumped up to next week's agenda. This practice was very demoralizing for me. I felt as if I never reached the end. I, like so many of us, was expecting too much of myself.

Shorten that work order to a few necessary and realistic accomplishments and enjoy a sense of satisfaction and closure as you successfully cross through each task.

As parents, we want so badly for our children to be their best, act their best and look their best that we become too intense. All perspective is lost. We often seek to be in control of situations and circumstances to protect our children from being hurt or disappointed. Unfortunately, the more intense and controlling we become, the more distant, uncooperative and resentful our children become.

I remember an incident with a parent of a fourth grade girl. The mother was extremely upset when she came into my office. She was at a loss about what to do with her daughter, Maggie. Their relationship was deteriorating rapidly. Her child hardly spoke to her, and when she did, the exchange was not pleasant. She sat down and began to relate her story.

Maggie absolutely hated going to dance class on Tuesday afternoons. So, every Tuesday around 3:30, a horrible fight ensued as mom attempted to transport Maggie to her lesson. Mother was determined that her daughter would honor her commitment and stay in the program for the school year. She explained that commitment was an important value in their family, and she felt adamant about instilling it in her child. I replied that I also felt commitment was a vital concept for children to embrace. However, her relationship with Maggie was even more crucial. I suggested that she sit down with Maggie and reinforce how strongly she felt about keeping commitments, but stress also that she cared even more about Maggie's feelings. In this case, Maggie's abhorrence for dance class was making both of them miserable.

As an alternative to simply allowing Maggie to drop dance class and "vegetate in front of the television" (mom's concern), we devised a slightly different plan of action. They would hold those two hours open and replace dance lessons with special together-time for the two of them.

We brainstormed and developed a list of projects and fun-filled adventures for mother and daughter. They would plan to go skating, bake a cake, plant a garden and go to the zoo!

By lightening up, this parent was able to salvage her relationship with her daughter. The new plan proved to be a boost to their self-esteems and, additionally, built a stronger bond between mother and child.

William Glaser, the guru of Reality Therapy says one of the most crucial safeguards our children can possess as adolescents is a healthy relationship with a parent. He believes that if a child holds a parent in high regard , the image of that parent will flash before him and serve as a powerful deterrent to dangerous behavior.

Parents must begin to foster this relationship of love and trust early. Adolescence is not the time to begin the process.

* * *

Be flexible, realistic and gentle with yourself and with your loved ones. It's okay to lighten-up. You will feel better about yourself, and your family will also reap the benefits. A wise person once said, "Don't sweat the small stuff, and it's almost all small stuff."

"Unrealistic expectations are the seedbed of depression."

– Zig Ziglar

"We need goals that are appropriate and attainable. Unrealistically high expectations steal the beauty and joy from our achievements."

– California task force to promote self-esteem and personal and social responsibility

"Strong feelings of self-esteem fuel a child's ability to learn to love, and to create."

– Ellie Kahn

"The internal combustion engine runs on gasoline, so the person runs on self-esteem: If he is full of it, he is good for the long run; if he is partly filled, he will soon need to be refueled; and if he is empty, he will come to a stop."

– Thomas Szasy

Chapter 4

• • • • • • • • • • • •

Step 3:
Spend Quality
Time

Step 3:
Spend Quality Time
•••••••••••

Once we have accented our lives with a "lighter" seasoning, it will be easy to progress to the third stage of this self-enhancement smorgasbord!

Spend some quality time with yourself. Most of us write our weekly list of "to do's,"careful to include and prioritize all areas of responsibility. Our job, our family, the house, groceries, bills, our church and even our community usually appear somewhere on the agenda. Who is often blatantly absent from our tally? We leave ourselves and our needs off of our list. At day's end, we are lucky to be left with just a few of the "table scraps."

You were going to take that walk yesterday and the day before, but time ran out and so did daylight. You have been wanting to go to that new restaurant for dinner, but by the time Friday rolls around, you are exhausted. The children have so many activities after school and on the weekends that luxuriating for an hour in a bath full of bubbles is a joke!

We repeatedly put ourselves and our well-being at the end of our schedule of activities and chores. In doing so, an unconscious message echoes over and over in our brains, "I must not be worth very much attention, I do not deserve to be pampered."

Place yourself and your needs at the top of the page in your daytimer. Put a new message on your internal recorder. "I am worthwhile and special. I deserve to spend at least one hour a day on myself." How do you feel when a friend takes the time to call and inquire about your well-being? When a loved one sends a card or flowers, you feel special.

Well, how about extending those same courtesies to yourself?

As I mentioned in Chapter 2, take a walk, read a few chapters in your favorite book, get a massage, window shop without feeling guilty for "wasting" time. Building self-esteem is never a waste. In fact, you will find that you have more energy and are in much better spirits. Then, everyone wins!

Children respond in the same way. We seem to be immersed in a "hurry-up, drop-off generation." Parents are consumed with job responsibilities that dictate long hours. Hence, children spend quite a few hours away from their parents. Once reunited at home, the routine is hectic and nerves are frayed. Special, quiet time with each other is lost among the demands of homework, dinner, television, baths, bills, and sleep.

Ink in at least thirty minutes a night for quality time with your children, separate from dinner time and homework help. Read a story, play a game, ride bikes, shoot baskets. This attention sends a very significant message to your children, "I must be pretty special and fun to be around because mom and dad take time out of their busy life to be with me exclusively." In his best seller, *Raising Positive Kids In A Negative World*, Zig Ziglar, well-known motivational speaker and author says "For a child, love is spelled T- I- M- E!"

* * *

Exclusive time spent with yourself and with your children is an investment in image-building that will yield valuable rewards for each participant!

"When we love something, it is of value to us, and when something is of value to us we spend time with it, time enjoying it and time taking care of it. So it is when we love children; we spend time admiring them and caring for them. We give them our time."

– M. Scott Peck, MD

"A strong awareness that you are loved by God provides the most solid foundation for building high self-esteem."

– Nido Qubein

"The last of the human freedoms is the ability to choose one's own attitude in any given set of circumstances, to choose one's own way."

– Viktor Frankl

Chapter 5

● ● ● ● ● ● ● ● ● ● ● ●

Step 4:
Reframe

Step 4:
Reframe
● ● ● ● ● ● ● ● ● ● ●

The fourth step toward embracing ourselves in a more positive way involves the skill of reframing.

Reframing is simply the act of changing a negative experience into a positive one. Whenever possible, reframe a situation or a behavior in a positive "picture frame."

By changing our frame of reference or our perception of an experience, we may even begin to view a supposed failure in a different light. Rather than falling off a cliff, so to speak, we have merely hit a speed bump in the road. Once we are able to see failure as merely an outcome or a result of a method that did not work, we can begin to treat it as a growing, learning adventure and move on!

Colonel Sanders of Kentucky Fried Chicken fame retired and discovered that he could not live comfortably on what he received from Social Security. Friends who had tasted his fried chicken encouraged him to market his recipe. He made literally hundreds of calls to companies and to individuals trying to sell his product. He finally met with success on his one thousand and first attempt. Someone is reported to have asked him how he kept from getting terribly discouraged as the rejections and failures continued to mount. He replied that he did not view his numerous sales approaches as failures but rather as learning opportunities. With each rejection, he learned another sales technique that did not work.

Reframing requires creative thinking, but, with practice, it quickly becomes a habit. Looking for the positive side to every experience soon occurs automatically. When our minds begin to practice positive thinking, our self-esteem improves by leaps and bounds!

Reframers are those people who seem to always exhibit a bright, sunny outlook on life!

President Ronald Reagan was an extremely talented reframer in the political arena. During a debate with his political opponent, Walter Mondale, Mr. Reagan was asked if he felt age would be an issue in the upcoming Presidential election. The "Great Communicator" replied that he had no intention of making an issue of Mondale's youth and inexperience. He had skillfully reframed the matter of his advanced age into a positive frame of experience and wisdom.

If practiced often, this skill will become second nature. You will find yourself immediately conducting a mental search for the good in every event. Once you become at ease with this talent, teach it to your children. You will be surprised how quickly they too will internalize the process. They will begin reframing for themselves, applying it to their own life-situations.

A youth soccer coach might model reframing to his young athletes in the following manner, "They may have scored more goals than we did, but we passed the ball much better and were stronger on defense. We will work on shooting in practice this week and will score more points in our next game." Instead of complaining that his players did not score enough, he reframed a lost game by complementing their passing and their defensive superiority.

I once worked with a teacher who was an expert at reframing. Children in her class felt great about themselves! She was able to transform many negative behaviors by using this technique.

One particular little boy comes to mind. Scott was a seven year old child who had a problem with lying or "telling stories." We were just one week into the new school year when his teacher came to my office. She was very upset about this little boy in her class who always told lies. She became even more distraught as she relayed the bizarre stories he had concocted.

The young teacher continued her visits to my office daily. With each drop-in, her rage and frustration intensified. Scott was a "pathological liar" by day two. He was "emotionally disturbed, belonged in a special class." He was "unable to distinguish between reality and fantasy and showed no remorse for the horrible untruths he offered." She even predicted that he would be a juvenile delinquent by middle school.

I must admit, he did spin some fantastic tales! He discovered plane crashes on the playground at recess and often angered the teacher and frightened the other students with the gory details. He could colorfully describe each of the wild, vicious animals that lived in his garage.

His teacher wanted him tested immediately and removed from the regular classroom. Two weeks had passed. The child and teacher were clashing so frequently that it became counterproductive to leave him in her class. Scott's self-worth was on a downward spiral, and the teacher was a nervous wreck.

Scott was moved to another class. I braced myself and waited for his new teacher to appear at my door. After just two days, she indeed did come to see me. I took a deep breath, fully expecting to be hit with a barrage of similar complaints.

She began, in a loud voice, "I cannot believe this child you have given me! He is, without a doubt, the most creative, imaginative student I have ever had the privilege to teach." She continued, exuberant and bubbling as she spoke. "He tells the most wonderful make-believe stories! I'm teaching him how to keep a journal to record all of his fables along with illustrations."

She even encouraged him to share some of his unique yarns with the class. She gently helped him understand the difference between real and make-believe, and all was well.

Scott's behavior did not change from teacher number one to teacher number two. He was still telling the same outrageous stories. But teacher number two reframed Scott's behavior into a positive frame. What was previously called pathological and disturbed had been lovingly redefined as creative and imaginative.

Needless to say, Scott flourished under the tutelage of his new teacher, and his self-esteem soared to new

Pathological Liar
Disturbed
Delinquent

Creative
Imaginative
Gifted

heights! In fact, this child who just a few weeks earlier was destined for a life of crime and failure, was tested for the gifted program and easily qualified.

Use reframing when your child brings his papers home for you to review. If he has a minus five written in bright red ink at the top of his paper, ignore it. Instead concentrate on the twenty questions he answered correctly.

It is our natural instinct to zero in on the incorrect responses. Try reframing, only discuss and praise the number answered correctly. Let your child tell you all about his right responses. By giving positive attention for the pluses and disregarding the minuses, you are offering an incentive to strive for more items in the plus column next time.

Of course, if you notice a pattern in his incorrect answers indicating a weakness in a certain area, that gap should be addressed later in a positive way. For instance, if all five questions that were marked in red dealt with multiplication, a review with a flash card game would reinforce those skills.

It *always* feels so much better to be lauded for what we have done well, than chastised for our shortcomings.

Dorothy Corkille Briggs, author of *Your Child's Self-Esteem*, says, "A positive identity hinges on positive life experiences."

* * *

Reframing encourages us to search for and discover the positive side of all life-experiences, even those that appear to be completely negative!

"Whether you believe you can or you can't, you're right!"

– Henry Ford

"For as a man thinketh in his heart, so is he."

– Proverbs 23:7

"The greatest discovery of my generation is that a human being can alter his life by altering his attitudes of mind."

– William James

"Our life is what our thoughts make it."

– Marcus Aurelius

"You can change by changing the way you think about yourself and your circumstances."

– Zig Ziglar

"When you have high self-esteem...you approach every moment, every event, every interaction with an attitude of openness instead of fear, giving instead of taking, acknowledging your strengths instead of weaknesses."

– Steven W. Vannoy

"Everything is possible for him who believes."

– Mark 9:23

"If you really want to be up in life, look for the good."

– Zig Ziglar

"The habit of looking on the best side of every event is worth more than a 1000 pounds a year."

– Samual Johnson

"It is the mind that maketh good or ill, that maketh wretch or happy, rich or poor."

– Edmund Spenser

Chapter 6

• • • • • • • • • • • •

Step 5:
Positive
Communication

Step 5:
Positive Communication
•••••••••••

I f I told you that I had a miracle product that was
guaranteed to boost self-esteem to new heights and,
as an added bonus, also improve relationships, you
would probably want to hear more about it. Well, positive
communication is the ingredient in this self-enhancement
recipe which achieves both of these enviable goals.

The word, communication, immediately conjures up im-
ages of people talking to each other. Communication is,
indeed, the act of relaying our thoughts, feelings, ideas and
needs to another person. We usually communicate with
words, but our body language and expressions can also trans-
mit our intentions and attitudes very effectively. What we
say and how we say it has a tremendous impact on our self-
worth and that of the person with whom we are speaking.

There is another kind of communication which has
the power to either catapult our self-confidence to unbe-
lievable heights or drag us down to the depths of self-hate.
It is self-communication or self-talk. The critiques and
comments we save for ourselves are usually much more
demeaning and cruel than those we bestow on others.
So, as we progress through this chapter, keep in mind
that positive communication is vital to self-esteem
whether we are talking to others or simply engaging in a
little self-talk!

"Make it a habit to say nice things about yourself, to yourself. You'll find that you like yourself better."

– Nido Quebin

**The art of positive communication
involves four key skills.**

I. Active-Reflective Listening

The most important but by far most difficult step on the blueprint for successful communication involves the skill of listening—Active-Reflective listening! The "active" part of this phrase means listening to and really hearing the thoughts and feelings behind the words.

So often when someone is talking to us, our mind is on a million other things. We distance ourselves, drifting off in the middle of the conversation. My husband can listen to me tell a story and, at the same time, be reading the sports page and clicking the remote control. He will

give me an occasional nod or "uh huh," but he isn't really listening actively to what I'm saying. I want him to be so interested in me and in what I am saying that nothing else matters. When he isn't, my feelings are hurt.

We have all done our share of passive listening and also recognize all too well when someone is not really hearing us. To actively listen, we must focus completely and exclusively on the person talking. Keep eye contact and make a concerted effort to screen out other distractions inside and outside of our minds. If it's appropriate, lean forward toward the person talking and even touch him. Really try to hear what the person is thinking and feeling.

After listening actively to the thoughts and feelings behind the words, it is then time to reflect them back to the speaker. We can repeat, paraphrase or interpret what we have heard. One way or another, give his thoughts and feelings back to him. This sends some very significant messages to the person who is talking:

1. "He is really listening and understanding what I'm saying. I know this because he has just repeated it back to me."

2. "I must be very important to him because he has dropped everything just to listen to me. He must think I'm pretty special!"

3. When the person speaking has a problem or need that he is discussing with you, by reflecting his thoughts and feelings back, you are sending the message that you feel he is capable of solving the problem himself.

You are not attempting to fix it or give advice. You are allowing him to stay with the feelings and thoughts long enough to work through the situation himself. Active-reflective listening not only helps both parties feel better about themselves but it also builds stronger relationships.

When you have a problem or are upset about a situation, what really makes you feel better? Does it ease your distress to be told what you need to do, or are you more comforted by just talking about your feelings with someone who listens in a caring way?

Society sends the message daily that pain or bad feelings of any kind are not acceptable. If you have a headache, take an aspirin; if you are depressed, take an antidepressant. The crucial point that seems to prevail is that discomfort must be eliminated immediately. By doing this, we fail to stay with the pain long enough to figure out the cause or to understand the origin. We often "stuff" the problem away only to have it resurface in other forms, such as physical ailments, stress, depression, fatigue or difficulties with sleeping and eating.

I once sat in on a drug recovery therapy group. Each of the participants was a recovering drug addict, and each had also attempted suicide at least once. Their biggest problem was being able to stay with their bad feelings long enough to work through them and deal with them. Their solutions to hurtful experiences in the past included taking drugs or trying to end their lives. A failed relationship, a lost job, an illness all precipitated that "quick fix" response. The therapist's most difficult task during the session was making them stay with uncomfortable feelings long enough to examine them and attempt to reconcile them. One girl started crying while sharing her experience and immediately began apologizing profusely for breaking down and showing such emotion and "weakness." Having crummy feelings occasionally is not a sign of weakness! It is OKAY!

Unfortunately though, we often relay this philosophy to our children by our responses to their problems and to their "unacceptable" behavior. In our desire to rescue our offspring from hurtful events, we forego active-reflective listening for other less effective methods. We advise, fix, deny, diminish and shame.

When Johnny comes home from school, slams the door, throws down his books and screams, "I hate school, I hate my teacher and I'm never going back," our first inclination is to make his unhappiness go away. It is very painful to see our child suffering. Some of our typical responses might be:

The fix-it response — "I will just call Mrs. Smith right now and get to the bottom of this!"

The advice response — "This is what you need to do. Go right up to the teacher tomorrow and tell her...etc."

The guilt response — "Shame on you for talking like that about school and your nice teacher." or "You know how it hurts mommy to see you angry, and I will not tolerate screaming and slamming doors."

The diminishing, denial response — In our effort to soothe, we often diminish or deny that a problem exists at all. "Now you know you love school. Why just yesterday you told me how nice your teacher was to you. Just go outside and play. You will soon forget all about it."

Each one of these responses will shut down the lines of communication immediately. You will never find out from little Johnny what happened at school. Even worse, Johnny goes away from this encounter feeling even less worthwhile than when he first stormed into the house. We have fixed, advised, denied, diminished and shamed with the best of intentions, but that is not what Johnny needed.

Now, let's replay the scene using active-reflective listening. When Johnny stomps in, slams the door, throws

his books and says, " I hate school, I hate my teacher and I'm never going to school again," you respond with, "Sounds like you had a really bad day at school today." "You bet I did, I hate Mrs. Smith." Johnny replies. You then reflect, "You are really mad at your teacher!" "Yeah" says Johnny, "you would be too, she doesn't like me anymore." Lovingly you question, "You feel like she no longer cares about you?" Johnny knows you are on his wavelength now and is eager to tell you more. "She doesn't care about me, she likes Sara and Joey better." "You feel like your teacher likes some of the other children more than she likes you." "She does, Mom." Johnny sadly admits. "Why, she let them go out to recess, and they got bad grades on their test too. I had to skip recess and redo my test. It's not fair."

You still may not solve the problem, but that is not really the point. The end goal is to keep the communication going long enough for him to work through his feelings and get them off his chest. He knows that you care and understand because you have listened actively and reflected his thoughts and feelings back to him.

When we are upset, all any of us really want is to have someone care enough to listen to us and offer a shoulder to lean on. When you come home from work, distraught by something your boss has done or said, do you expect your spouse or friend to give you advice or correct the situation? No, in most cases, you instead need a good listening ear while you vent your frustrations. Which response in the following scenario would tend to make you feel better?

"I am sick and tired of the way my boss treats me. He expects me to be a mind reader and yells at me if I don't anticipate his every wish. I think I am going to quit!"

Response #1 — "Oh stop being so sensitive. Go take a walk, you'll get over it."

Response # 2 — "Wow, it sounds like you are really having a bad time of it at work."

Obviously, the second, active-reflective answer sends a warm, caring message and coaxes you to continue talking.

* * *

Active-reflective listening not only develops more positive relationships, it also encourages feelings of self-worth and self-confidence.

"It is the disease of not listening, the malady of not marking, that I am troubled withal."

– William Shakespeare

"Proof of understanding comes only with active listening."

– Dorothy Corkille Briggs

"The first duty of love is to listen."

– Paul Tillich

"People ought to listen more slowly."

– Jean Sparks Ducey

"Good listeners don't interrupt – ever – unless the house is on fire."

– Letitia Baldrige

"Most of us are only tuned in to distant stations where all kinds of things are happening to other people. We listen through the static to their heartbreaks as if we were in some well-protected receiving chamber."

– Jonathon Schwartz

"Parents can learn to avoid such hazards to effective communication. They can learn to listen attentively and respond succinctly and sympathetically."

– Haim G. Ginott

"The parent who doesn't listen is implying that what his or her child feels, thinks and says is not particularly important. Such a message can be a blow to a teen's often shaky self-esteem."

– Kathleen McCoy

II. Me Language

The specific words we use with each other and with ourselves have such a tremendous impact on self-esteem. Me Language gets the point across and preserves everyone's dignity! When someone else's behavior or a situation someone else has created is causing a problem for you, Me Language works wonders. It has many more sophisticated and complicated relatives — assertive communication, I messages and nondirective communication. However, I believe Me language is the simplest and most positive vehicle for stating and rectifying a problem.

Me Language simply tells another person how something he has done or said makes you feel and what you would like done about it. Sounds effortless, doesn't it? Well, there is one catch; you have to do this without using the word, YOU!

When the word "you" is used in a confrontational or critical manner, it becomes a blaming word that elicits feelings of anger, defiance, rebellion and hurt. It also always diminishes self-esteem in the process. "Me Language" is a valuable skill to learn. It takes practice, but once you have mastered it, you will be able to let your feelings be known and change the unpleasant situation without causing hurt or anger.

If you have children, you have certainly struggled at some time or another with the "messy room" scenario. Let me give you two examples of an encounter with teen-

age Susie regarding this hot topic! The first interchange demonstrates blaming "you" language.

"Susie, you are driving me crazy. You are such a slob! Look at the way you have wrecked your room. You have no respect for anything. You throw your clothes and books all over the floor, and you never bother to take the dirty dishes down to the kitchen. You are just plain lazy and defiant. You have been told over and over to clean your room. Why don't you listen to me?"

In that short paragraph, I used the word <u>you</u> nine times. In the process of letting Susie know how I felt about her room, I also demeaned and attacked her person and her worth. In doing so, I have also encouraged Susie to be even more obstinate and resentful toward me. We both leave the confrontation upset and certainly do not feel very positive about ourselves.

Me language has the power to turn an adversarial conversation into a nonthreatening, factual statement.

By inserting this unique method of communicating into the Susie story, a whole new mood is created.

"Susie, when I walk past this room, I get so upset. I see clothes and books thrown all over the floor and dirty dishes that need to be put in the dishwasher. I have asked many times today that this room be cleaned. I am going to come back past this room in thirty minutes. I expect the clothes to be hung in the closet, the books put away on the shelf and the dishes placed in the dishwasher."

I delivered the same basic message about how the messy room made me feel without using the word you and without destroying Susie's self-worth.

My rage over the condition of the room was kept completely separate from her value as a person.

The room still might not get cleaned to my satisfaction, but her self-esteem and our relationship have been saved. Ten years from now, the tension over an untidy room will be long forgotten, but how she feels about herself and the quality of this relationship will be extremely important.

* * *

Use me language in all areas of your life. It creates an atmosphere of cooperation and congeniality and makes everyone involved feel more positive and confident.

Remember self-talk! Leave out those negative, blaming "yous" when you are displeased with your own performance too!

"Abusive adjectives attached to personality have a devastating effect."

– Haim G. Ginott

"Of all the traps and pitfalls in life, self-disesteem is the deadliest, and the hardest to overcome, for it is a pit designed and dug by our own hands, summed up in the phrase, 'it's no use – I can't do it.' You can do the impossible."

– Maxwell Maltz

III. Praise and Criticism

Me language focuses on a behavior or a situation rather than the character or worth of the person involved. This principle is vital for building healthy relationships with others and for enhancing our own self-image. We should always take great care to separate what a person does from who he is. This standard applies to criticism and to praise. Praise and criticize the deed not the doer, the artwork not the artist. When we entangle behavior with identity, we tie in self-worth with achievements and failures.

It is so easy as parents to connect our love to our children's accomplishments. On seeing Tommy's outstanding report card, a well meaning father might say, as he gives him a hug, "I love you so much for getting straight A's." That seems like a harmless comment,

doesn't it? But Tommy may mistakenly interpret dad's enthusiasm as meaning he loves him because he achieved A's. Now the pressure is on for Tommy. If he fails to do as well next time, will he be jeopardizing his father's love? Instead of praising in that manner, dad might first assure him of his unconditional love and then address the report card: "I love you, and it makes me happy when you do so well in school."

Sara is not mean for hitting her younger sister. Hitting her sister is mean. Bobby is not a good boy because he shared his toys with his cousin. He is a good and special child just because "he is" and sharing his toys with his cousin is "a good thing to do."

A first grade boy was once sent to my office. The teacher was at her wits end. Chris repeatedly threw rocks at other children during recess. When I asked him what he was thinking as he threw rocks, he sadly exclaimed that he did it because he was a "bad boy." He went on to explain that he had been bad all of his life (all six years) and that was why he did things he should not do.

Chris and I worked for many weeks trying to undo his negative opinion of himself. My task was to convince him that his actions were sometimes bad, but he was always good and worthwhile.

Of course, the adults in his life also needed to change their manner of communicating with him. His mother was understandably frustrated. She was a young, single mother with no previous childrearing experience. Chris was a rambunctious little boy who craved attention, and he was smart enough to know that bad behavior would get attention!

Mom found herself constantly repeating those degrading phrases: "You are a bad boy, you are mean, you are inconsiderate, you are wild, terrible, and on and on and on....." Once she began to address his behavior as completely separate from who and what he was, Chris' opinion of himself slowly changed. He began to believe he was worthwhile. Soon an amazing thing began to happen! As Chris' self-esteem improved, his inappropriate behaviors started to disappear!

Self-talk

At the beginning of this chapter, I referred to the term, self-talk. We can quickly demoralize ourselves by tearing away at our image — one word or phrase at a time!

If I blow a speech, I am not a "bad speaker," I simply made a bad speech. If I feel like I made a bad impression at an important business dinner, "I am not stupid and inept"; my performance was just not up to par at that particular event.

Women tend to be especially hard on themselves during self-communication. "I'm ugly, I'm fat, I'm old, I'm stupid." Sound familiar? If we tell ourselves something long enough, like little Chris, we too begin to believe it.

* * *

Practice making only positive statements to and about yourself and critique only your behavior. You will be pleasantly surprised at how quickly your self-worth and your performance escalate to new heights. You will also be providing a wonderful model for your children to copy.

"A child valued for who she is has the best chance for true self-esteem."

– Ava L. Siegler

"When young people assume that parents are concerned only with how well they do, rather than with who they are, the need to achieve becomes addictive."

– David Elkind

"Most people do not believe what they do matters because they have low self-esteem. It is our job as leaders to help them realize their self-worth and build their self-esteem through recognition and reinforcement of their value to the organization."

– Ray Leone

"Praise that evaluates personality or character is unpleasant and unsafe. Praise that describes efforts, accomplishments, and feelings is helpful and safe."

– Haim G. Ginott

IV. Be Specific

Talking to one another is such a natural, automatic process, yet a simple interchange between two people frequently leads to confusion, misunderstanding or hurt feelings.

Praise, criticism, directions and information are often so general that the recipient feels overwhelmed and bewildered. These uncomfortable feelings can be avoided by simply taking care to be specific in our communication.

When your five year old brings home a picture she drew in school, praise is definitely in order. However,

by exclaiming; "Wow you are a great artist, that is the best picture I have ever seen," you have probably left her wondering exactly what it is about the drawing that makes it so terrific. She may also be worrying if she will be able to live up to the title of "great artist" in the future. All of her doubt could be avoided by praising the picture specifically. "Wow, I really like the way you used so many different colors in this drawing. I can tell it must be fall, because the leaves are brown and orange. It must be a nice clear day too because the sun is shining so brightly in the sky!"

By telling your little Picasso in detail what you like about her creation, you have set the stage for another work of art. She knows now that she is very talented in her use of colors and in drawing the sun. You did not intertwine her ability to draw with her identity by telling her she was a great artist, but she knows you like her gift, and she will be eager to try again.

My son was a soccer player and my daughter was a swimmer. For years, I patted them on their backs or gave them hugs as I told them they played a great game or swam a super race. How much better it would have been for their self-confidence to have said, "You really kept your eye on the ball and played your position well. You were always in the right place to get the passes." Or, "Your stroke seemed so smooth. I noticed your kick was especially strong, and you took very few breaths." By being more precise with my praise, I would have given them a road map for future performances.

If my teacher or supervisor returned a report to me with "redo, this is unacceptable," written across the top,

I would most likely feel upset, frustrated and hurt. Obviously, I thought it was all right, or I would not have submitted it. This vague comment serves only to create confusion. Chances are I spent many hours completing that assignment, and I want to know what she dislikes and how she wants it changed.

All misunderstanding and confusion could have easily been avoided if she had simply stated, "I really appreciate your work on this project. I would like to suggest a few changes and additions, and it should be ready to resubmit. I would like for you to be more detailed and actually list the ideas you have for making the project work. Please double space so it will be easier to read, and leave more room in the margins for notes."

Now, she has stated exactly what she wants. With the initial instruction, I could be redoing the report over and over because there were no specific guidelines.

General criticism makes us feel generally incompetent and incapable.

Each one of us perceives things differently. A clean garage might present two totally different pictures to a parent and to a teenager.

Being clear and detailed when giving directions can save relationships, preserve self-esteem and prevent blowups!

If I tell my child to clean her room before going out to play, I am setting the stage for certain misperception. To a ten-year-old, cleaning her room might mean merely making the bed and piling all of her clothes, toys and trash in the closet. A problem then arises when the child sincerely believes she has completed the task adequately, and she is reprimanded for not doing what she was told. She feels betrayed and also feels like a failure. By being very specific with my directions, I could have prevented these undesirable consequences.

Clean Room

1. Dust Furniture

2. Vacuum Carpet

3. Hang Clothes In Closet

4. Clean Mirror

It is a good idea to actually make a step by step list of what needs to be done, "Please dust the furniture, vacuum the carpet, hang your clothes in the closet and clean the mirror."

If we know what is expected of us, we can proceed with confidence and, upon completion, have a sense of accomplishment in knowing we have done the job correctly.

At the beginning of this chapter, I said that positive communication was a miracle product that was guaranteed to boost self-esteem and improve relationships.

* * *

Practice the four techniques discussed in this section, and watch the miracle unfold in your life!

1. Active-reflective Listening

2. Me Language

3. Separate the behavior from the person.

4. Be specific.

They really do work!!!!

"Whenever personal worth is dependent upon performance, personal value is subject to cancellation with every misstep."

– Dorothy Corkille Briggs

"The real solvent of class distinction is a proper measure of self-esteem – a kind of unselfconsciousness. Some people are at ease with themselves – so the world is at ease with them."

– Alan Bennett

Chapter 7
• • • • • • • • • • •

Step 6:
Give
Unconditional
Love, Acceptance
And Respect

Unconditional Love

Unconditional Acceptance

Unconditional Respect

Step 6:
Give Unconditional Love, Acceptance And Respect
• • • • • • • • • • • •

The final seasoning in this savory recipe for a healthier self-esteem calls for a generous sprinkling of unconditional love, acceptance and respect.

For self-worth to thrive, we have to love, accept and respect ourselves unconditionally. The "unconditional" means without restrictions, exceptions or "ifs." The following are examples of conditional thought processes that will dilute this self-esteem formula and cause our image to sour.

1. "I'd be happy with myself if I could just lose 20 pounds."

2. "I won't feel like I'm a good salesperson until I make at least $10,000 more a year.

3. "My ideas probably are not as valuable as my co-workers, because I don't have a college degree."

We may wish we were 20 pounds thinner, made $10,000 more a year and had a college degree, but those wishes should not affect our self-love, acceptance or respect.

As self-serving as it may sound, we must love ourselves and take care of our physical, emotional and spiritual needs first. It is really very logical. If we do not genuinely like ourselves, then it would be presumptuous to expect others to be unconditional in their opinions and judgements of us.

As I mentioned in Chapter Four, our nurturing natures many times cause us to minister to the needs, wants and cares of others first. In doing so, we often neglect our own health and well being.

I remember being appalled by the words of the flight attendants the first few times I flew. During the safety briefing, the statement was made that in case of a loss of cabin pressure, oxygen masks would drop down. Then came that horrifying command, "If you are traveling with a small child, always place your mask securely on your face first and then take care of your child." I would mumble to myself in disbelief and silent defiance that no loving parent would ever neglect his child's safety and security while seeing to his own needs. I would certainly put the oxygen mask on my child first if an emergency ever occurred!

Soon, reason overpowered my mothering instinct, and the meaning of the attendant's directive was crystal clear. If I do not make sure I am able to breathe and think lucidly, I will be of no use to my child. Doesn't this principle hold true in all areas of our lives, on the ground as well as 30,000 feet in the air? Of course it does!

As the caregiver in your family, your first responsibility is to yourself. Get plenty of sleep, eat nutritiously, exercise and cater to your own emotional and spiritual necessities.

Then and only then will you have the energy, strength, motivation and courage to attend to the needs, wants, desires and worries of your loved ones. Vince Lombardi once said, "Fatigue makes cowards of us all." We must be operating at 100% to be of the greatest value to ourselves and to others.

Children observe and copy their parents' behaviors. By loving, accepting and respecting ourselves unconditionally, we model the importance of positive self-worth and the value of taking care of oneself. Our children will follow our example and treat themselves in a similar manner.

By communicating this same nonjudgmental attitude toward our children, we free them to create, risk and be themselves without fear of criticism and failure. They will have the courage to attempt new tasks and the self-confidence to succeed.

Many of us grew up in an atmosphere where undo importance was placed on conformity, stereotyped thinking, rigid order and compliance. Acceptance often depended on the outcome of our behavior. This type of environment certainly discourages high self-esteem and self-confidence.

We may not always like our children's actions, approve of their beliefs or agree with their likes and dislikes. It is imperative, however, that we continually demonstrate our total and unconditional love, acceptance and respect for them as the special human beings that they are.

My father gave me just such support during a very difficult and painful time in my life. There were so many decisions to be made, and each one seemed so confusing and overwhelming. One day, feeling completely exhausted and distraught, I asked his advice on an important matter. His reply touched my heart and buoyed my sinking self-worth. He simply said, "Billie, I love you and have complete confidence that the choice you make will be the right one for you. You have always done the correct thing, and I know you will this time." He then added, "Know that I will always support you and be 100% behind you whichever path you choose." Armed with both my mother's and father's absolute love, acceptance and respect, I garnered the strength to move on with my life.

* * *

Give these three gifts to yourself and to your family. Your own self-esteem will naturally blossom and the fragrance of that bloom will spread to those you love.

"Nonjudgemental, unconditional love is the most healing force in the world."

– C.A. Seguin

"Total, unconditional acceptance of yourself is the first step in building a positive self-image."

– Nido Quebin

"When children have learned through the love of their parents to feel valuable, it is almost impossible for the vicissitudes of adulthood to destroy their spirit."

– M. Scott Peck, MD

"Nobody holds a good opinion of a man who has a low opinion of himself."

– Anthony Trollope

"From a psychiatric point of view, I would say man's deepest flaw is to mistrust himself and to withhold love and self-acceptance."

– David Burns

"Through unconditional love, positivity, listening, and acceptance, we can give our children the tool of self-esteem"

– Scott L. Anderson

Chapter 8
• • • • • • • • • • • •

A
Brief Recap

A Brief Recap
• • • • • • • • • • •

I t is time now to blend all six ingredients together to create a new, enhanced, stronger self-esteem!

1. **Create and Maintain a Balance in Your Life.**
   Devote some time each day to all areas of development.

   A. Physical

   B. Emotional

   C. Social

   D. Spiritual

   E. Intellectual

2. **Lighten-up.**
   Remember to set reasonable goals, guidelines and rules.

   A. Be flexible

   B. Keep everything in perspective

3. **Spend Quality Time.**
   Spend quality and quantity time on yourself and with your loved ones. It sends an important message, "I am worthwhile!"

4. Reframe.

Try to reframe every negative experience or situation into a positive picture frame. By changing the way we look at something, we change how we feel about ourselves.

5. Positive Communication.

A. Use Active-reflective Listening. Listen to the thoughts and feelings behind the words, then reflect them back.

B. Use Me Language. Tell how you feel about a certain behavior or situation and what you would like done about it. Do this without using the blaming word, "YOU"!

C. Always separate the behavior from the person's worth. Praise or criticize the deed not the doer.

D. Be specific when praising, criticizing and giving directions.

6. Give unconditional love, acceptance and respect to yourself and to others.

Positive self-esteem is the catalyst which guides you toward greater happiness and success in all areas of life. A daily mixture of these six ingredients will nourish you with the strength, courage and energy needed to journey through each day feeling genuinely good about yourself! You will truly love the self-assured, capable and competent "you" that has evolved. This confidence and love will also bless and inspire everyone you touch!

"An individual's self-concept is the core of his personality. It affects every aspect of human behavior: the ability to learn, the capacity to grow and change, the choice of friends, mates and careers. It's no exaggeration to say that a strong positive self-image is the best possible preparation for success in life."

– Dr. Joyce Brothers

Bibliography

Berne, Pat & Savary, Lou. *Building Self-Esteem in Children.* New York, N.Y.: Crossroad Publishing Co., 1985.

Branden, Nathaniel. *The Psychology of Self-Esteem.* Los Angeles, CA: Nash Publishing, 1969.

Briggs, Dorothy Corkville. *Celebrate Yourself.* Garden City, N.Y.: Doubleday & Co., 1977.

Briggs, Dorothy Corkille. *Your Child's Self-Esteem.* Garden City, N.Y.: Doubleday, 1970.

Burwickl, Ray. *Self-Esteem: You're Better Than You Think.* Weaton, IL: Tyndale, 1983.

Canfield, Jack & Wells, Harold C. *100 Ways to Enhance Self-Concept in the Classroom.* Englewood Cliffs, N.J.: Prentice-Hall, Inc., 1976.

Clarke, Jean Illsley. *Self-Esteem: A Family Affair.* New York, N.Y.: Harper & Row, 1978.

Clemes, Harris & Bean, Reynold. *How to Raise Children's Self-Esteem.* Los Angeles, CA: Price, Stern, Sloan, 1978.

Clemes, Harris & Bean, Reynold. *Self-Esteem.* New York, N.Y.: G.P. Putnam's Sons, 1987.

Elkind, David. *The Hurried Child.* Reading, Massachusetts: Addison-Wesley Publishing, 1988.

Ginott, Haim G. *Between Parent and Child.* New York, N.Y.: Macmillan, 1968.

Maloney, Raymond. *How To Cure Low Self-Esteem.* Novato, CA: Ann Arbor Publications, 1986.

Peck, M. Scott M.D. *The Road Less Traveled.* New York, N.Y.: Simon & Schuster Publishing, 1978.

Schuller, Robert H. *Self-Esteem,The New Reformation.* Waco, Texas: Word Books, 1982.

Smalley, Gary & Trent, John Ph.D. *The Blessing.* New York, N.Y.: Pocket Books, 1986.

Vannoy, Steven W. *The 10 Greatest Gifts I Give My Children*, New York, NY: Simon & Schuster, 1994.

Wellingham-Jones, Patricia. *Adolescence and Self-Esteem.* Tehama, CA: Wellingham-Jones, 1984.

Zig Ziglar. *Raising Positive Kids In A Negative World.* Nashville, TN: Thomas Nelson Publishers, 1985.

 **Yes** I want to share this book with others!

SEND THIS FORM
ALONG WITH PAYMENT TO:

Billie Bacon
P O Box 62673
N. Charleston, S. C. 29419-2673

Or Call: 1-800-884-5780

	Qty	Each	Amount
One Deluxe Order Of **Healthy Self-Esteem To Go!!** *An easy to follow recipe for positive self-esteem.*		$11.95	
		Sub Total	
Please add $3 shipping & handling for 1 book and $1 s/h for each additional book.		S/H	
		TOTAL	

(Quantity discounts are available on bulk purchases)

Name _____ Date _____

Company _____ E-mail _____

Street Address _____

City/Province _____ State _____

Zip/Postal Code _____ Country _____ Phone _____

☐ *VISA.* ☐ *MasterCard* ☐ Check/Money Order (Payable to Billie Bacon)

Card
No. / / / / / / / / / / / / / / / / / /

Exp.
date _____ Signature _____